Jacqueline Harris

# Write your own BOOK

Design your own cover.

To design your cover, turn the page and fold out the flap.

DK

# Contents

## Important note for you!

Do you know what you want to write stories about, or have no idea at all? Whichever, this book will INSPIRE you to write your own stories. It will help you sort out your ideas or give you some different ideas altogether.

ENJOY YOURSELF! WRITING IS A LOT OF FUN AND I HOPE YOU HAVE A GREAT TIME WRITING YOUR OWN BOOK.

This book begins with lots of ACTIVITIES for trying out different types of writing and developing storytelling skills. These can be done in any order.

**CHALLENGE!**
Use at least 2 similes and 2 metaphors in the description. For example, simile – it charged like a torpedo; it is as huge as a house; metaphor – the claws are sharp daggers.

Pick a pet
Create an imaginary pet. It could be with amazing powers (a flying ham imaginary one (a unicorn). Sketch and write notes about your pet here...

**WORD BOX**
5 super-heroic alliteration words:
1. superb
2. stunning
3. sensational
4. spectacular
5. sprightly
Try another letter!

It also provides some helpful TIPS and TRICKS to make your writing better, such as examples of excellent words (or use your own) and writing challenges. It will be useful to have a dictionary and a thesaurus handy to search for and spell other fantastic words.

**IT'S TRUE!**
RSVP stands for 'répondez, s'il vous plaît', which is French for 'Please reply'.

An invitation
You are cordially invited to write invitation! Maybe it's to Cinde a dinner. Or maybe it's to the N him to a dinner party.

Remember to write the time, place and date of the event.

DISCOVER how to make your writing really interesting so that people will be excited to read it.

*Talking helps your ideas become clearer and inspires new ideas to try out.*

Look out for the TALKING POINTS. Most writers often find it very helpful to talk over ideas before they sit down to write. Talk through your ideas with family members or friends.

At the end of the book, there are pages for writing your own FULL-LENGTH STORY. You'll be amazed at what you think up!

# Framing a fairy tale

Once upon a time, in a land far, far away, a fantastical story is about to unfold…. Write your own short fairy tale, thinking carefully about how it is structured.

Write how the story begins here.

Who will your main character be?

## Once upon a time,

In which mystical land will your tale be set?

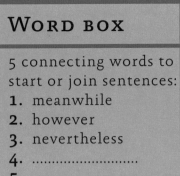
Keep your story flowing by linking together short sentences and using dramatic language to amaze, terrify or delight your reader.

Make the middle part exciting.

𝕿𝖍𝖊 𝕰𝖓𝖉

What obstacles will your character overcome?

Will there be a happy ending?

# Into the jungle

Imagine you are peering through the dense trees of a jungle. What do you see? Use your own drawings to complete the scene.

Colour the picture.

Add plenty of plants and animals.

Now write two paragraphs
to describe your scene.

**WORD BOX**

5 words to create
the atmosphere in
the jungle:
1. humid
2. overgrown
3. swampy
4. .........................
5. .........................
   Add your own.

*How will your description make someone feel like they are in the jungle?*

*What do the animals look like?*

# Heroes

When the bank is being robbed or the city is in danger – who will save the day?

How will your hero know when help is needed?

Draw your own hero here.

Will your hero have an outfit or disguise?

Characters

5 super-heroic
alliteration words:
1. superb
2. stunning
3. sensational
4. spectacular
5. sprightly
   Try another letter!

How will your hero stop a villain from getting away? Do they have any gadgets? Does your hero have a sidekick to help them?

*What makes your hero extraordinary?*

*If you could have a superpower, what would it be?*

Describe something amazing your hero has done.

# Lights, camera, action!

What's your favourite movie? How does it start? Does the story jump smack, bang into the middle of the action? If you made a movie, how would it begin?

**IT'S TRUE!**
Storytellers often use mystery and dramatic events to hook their readers and keep them interested.

Write the details of your movie on this clapperboard.

MOVIE TITLE:

DIRECTOR:

SCENE:

LOCATION:

Where is your movie set?

Who are your main characters and which actors would play them?

Write the opening scene of your movie.
How will you grab your audience's attention?

Your first sentence is key in
attracting your audience.

How will you introduce your characters?

What facts will you give your audience straight away?

# Jurassic encounter

Imagine you are in the time of the dinosaurs.
Look out! A pterodactyl is trying to dive-bomb you!

Write a description of a dinosaur using lots of adjectives.

Write your first dinosaur description on this page.

**IT'S TRUE!**
Antonyms are opposites and synonyms are words with the same meaning.

Is your dinosaur a plant-eater or a meat-eater?

Write the same description here but change all the adjectives to their antonyms.

**WORD BOX**

5 descriptive words and their antonyms:
1. huge/tiny
2. scaly/smooth
3. ferocious/timid
4. nimble/lumbering
5. powerful/weak
Try some others!

What colour is the dinosaur?

What effect do the new words have on the appearance of your dinosaur?

# An invitation

You are cordially invited to write your own fairy-tale invitation! Maybe it's to Cinderella, inviting her to a disco. Or maybe it's to the Big Bad Wolf, inviting him to a dinner party.

Remember to write the time, place and date of the event.

What will your event be? A birthday party or maybe a summer barbecue?

Decorate the border of the invitation with drawings or stickers.

Who else will you invite to your party?

Think of the dress code for this event. Will there be a theme?

Sketch some ideas of what you will wear and what other people may wear?

*What will you wear?*

*Will it be fancy dress for your guests?*

Label the different parts of the outfits.

# Pick-and-mix story

There are whole dictionaries filled with words for you to use when you write. Just a handful of random words could inspire a story.

Choose one word from each of the lists on this page.

bottle
letter
castle
forest
zebra
toothbrush
island
submarine

homework
bed
laptop
map
umbrella
message
thunder
backpack

elephant
pear
toy
kitten
shoebox
bucket
pillow
pizza

Are there things on the lists that would make a funny story?

WORD BOX

5 adjectives to use for
your chosen words:
1. flying
2. invisible
3. dangerous
4. ............................
5. ............................
   Add your own.

Can you make someone laugh with your story idea?

Plot your story with your
three chosen things.

How will you connect the three things in your story?

# Real settings

Think about a place that you know really well, such as your school or bedroom. It may be ordinary, but how could you make the place extraordinary?

How does this place smell?

Stick in a photograph or draw a picture of this place.

What objects are in the room?

What might make the place exciting to read about? Write a detailed description of the place to captivate a reader. For example, the place at night.

**WORD BOX**

5 ordinary to extraordinary words:
1. flat/rippled
2. large/gigantic
3. sharp/spiky
4. damp/steamy
5. shiny/shimmering
Try some others!

*What interesting words could make the place extraordinary?*

# Pick a pet

Create an imaginary pet. It could be a real animal with amazing powers (a flying hamster) or an imaginary one (a unicorn).

Sketch and write notes about your pet here.

Will it have a pattern on its body?

Will your pet have wings? How will it move?

How big will it be?

Describe your pet. Let the words paint a picture of the pet, so the reader can imagine exactly what it is like.

CHALLENGE!

Use at least 2 similes and 2 metaphors in the description. For example, simile – it charged like a torpedo; it is as huge as a house; metaphor – the claws are sharp daggers.

What will be extraordinary about your pet?

# Mix up magic

Double, double, toil and trouble; fire burn, and cauldron bubble! Create a magical spell. First write a list of ingredients and then write your method.

**WORD BOX**

5 adjectives to describe your ingredients:
1. stinky
2. gruesome
3. sticky
4. ..........................
5. ..........................
   Add your own.

Make a list of ingredients and how many of each you will need.

Is your spell nasty or nice; ghastly or good?

Use drawings to show what you'll add to your cauldron.

It's important that the instructions are clear.
Use words such as 'next' and 'then' in your method.

How long will it take
to prepare and cook?

Give your spell
a name.

Preparation: .........mins

Cooking: ........mins

Number your
instructions so
they are easier
to follow.

What is your spell for?

# Scary story

What sends chills down your spine and makes the hairs on the back of your neck stand on end?

Describe a scenario where your worst nightmare comes true.

**WORD BOX**

5 alarming adjectives:
1. evil
2. haunted
3. blood-curdling
4. creeping
5. poisonous
   Use a thesaurus to find some more.

Write a short, spooky tale to strike fear into the heart of your reader. What will give them goosebumps?

Will your story have ghouls and goblins or snakes and spiders?

When and where will it be set?

# Famous places

We don't need to travel the world to imagine what big cities are like. Looking at pictures can give us a good idea, for example, we get a sense that they are busy and noisy.

Choose a city. Find a picture of the place. Describe what the city is like.

What can you see, hear and smell?

What are the interesting things about the city and the different things you can do there?

Write a guide for tourists to make them want to visit.

Will you include information on places to shop and eat?

How will visitors get around: a tour; a taxi?

CHALLENGE!
Think of 5 ways that cities are different to the countryside.

What entertainment is there?

# Art of persuasion

The power of persuasion can be very useful to help cunning characters get their own way.

Who is your buyer?

Create an advert to sell a product of your choice.

Use pictures and powerful words.

What makes it an attractive product?

What are you trying to sell?

A travelling salesman has some magic beans to sell. Write what he might say to persuade you to buy them from him. Think about adverts you have seen.

CHALLENGE!
Try and use at least two of the following in your persuasive text: repeated words, emotional language, rhetorical questions, humour.

How are the beans magical?

What will make you want to buy the beans?

# Pundit practice

She shoots, she scores! The crowds are going wild! Describing the action within a story helps readers to picture the scene. Imagine you are a sports commentator watching an exciting game of your favourite sport.

 *Who is the best player?*

Draw a picture of the competitors or team players. Give them names.

### Competitors

**IT'S TRUE!**
A pundit is a person who offers their observations and opinions.

*What skills do the players need?*

Commentators need to be able to think fast and describe a moment in vivid detail. What words and phrases best describe action?

Describe an exciting moment in a sports game. Try and use words to convey the emotion and dramatic action.

How do the players move?

Do the players work well as a team?

# Letter writing

Rewrite a well known story in a different way. Imagine you are a fairy-tale character writing about your adventure.

Write a letter to another character and describe what has happened to you. For example, you could be Goldilocks writing to Baby Bear.

Is your story funny, scary or silly?

Dear _____

Use first person to describe events from your point of view.

Make sure you use the past tense.

This character is astonished by the story you told them in your letter. Write their reply here.

**WORD BOX**

5 past/present words with contractions:
1. don't/didn't
2. can't/couldn't
3. shan't/shouldn't
4. won't/wouldn't
5. isn't/wasn't

What words will best describe the character's surprise?

**Dear**
_____
_____
_____
_____
_____
_____
_____
_____
_____
_____
_____
_____
_____
_____
_____

Does the character offer advice?

# Word eruption!

A good story has something very exciting happening in the middle. Imagine you are next to a volcano that is about to erupt. Oh no! It's going to blow...

Continue the story. Make it as exciting as it can possibly be, but don't say how it ends.

Make sure to finish on a cliffhanger.

Can you describe the volcano and what is happening around you?

How can you make the story exciting?

Sketch and write notes about your volcano here.

**IT'S TRUE!**
In a cliffhanger, the words take the reader right up to the edge of a huge, scary cliff, and then stop, leaving them hanging.

What can you hear, feel, smell and see?

# Castle adventure

Begin an adventure set in a castle. Draw and label your castle. Add as much detail to your picture as you can.

What materials were used to make your castle?

What is going on in each part of the castle?

Imagine you are a knight's squire or a maid, or on a school trip, writing about your visit to the castle. Is it happening now or in the past?

CHALLENGE!
Use complex sentences and try to extend them, e.g. *The giant stone walls towered over me, making me feel as small as an ant.*

What do you see at the castle?

What happens? How does it make you feel?

# Villains

Villains are the bad characters in a story.

How would you describe these villians? What crimes have they committed?

**WANTED**

## MR MONOCLE

£500,000 for the capture of this monocled master criminal, who has disclosed national state secrets. Also wanted for smuggling.

**REWARD**

NOTORIOUS OUTLAW
THE LONE WOLF!

£100,000 DEAD OR ALIVE!

Wanted for eating little pigs. Contact: Watson's Detective Agency and Dangerous Animals Welfare Services.

**REWARD**

☞ $10,000 ☜
IN GOLD COINS!

Wanted for robbery, murder and other crimes. Contact the sheriff if you have any information.

**WANTED**

Woman in black; Jewel thief extraordinaire! Stolen jewels worth more than £2 million

REWARD
£50,000

Trained as a Ninja warrior. Do not approach! This woman is extremely dangerous. May not work alone.

Design a wanted poster for a villain.
Create your own character or use
one from a story.

Include a picture,
a description and details
of the crime committed.

Is there a reward?

Which story villains do you know?

# Expressing emotions

Throughout our lives, we experience many kinds of feelings. Some are good, such as feeling happy, excited, safe or relaxed. Others are bad, such as feeling angry, jealous, sad or scared.

Look at the following pictures. Can you read these faces? Describe how you think these people are feeling?

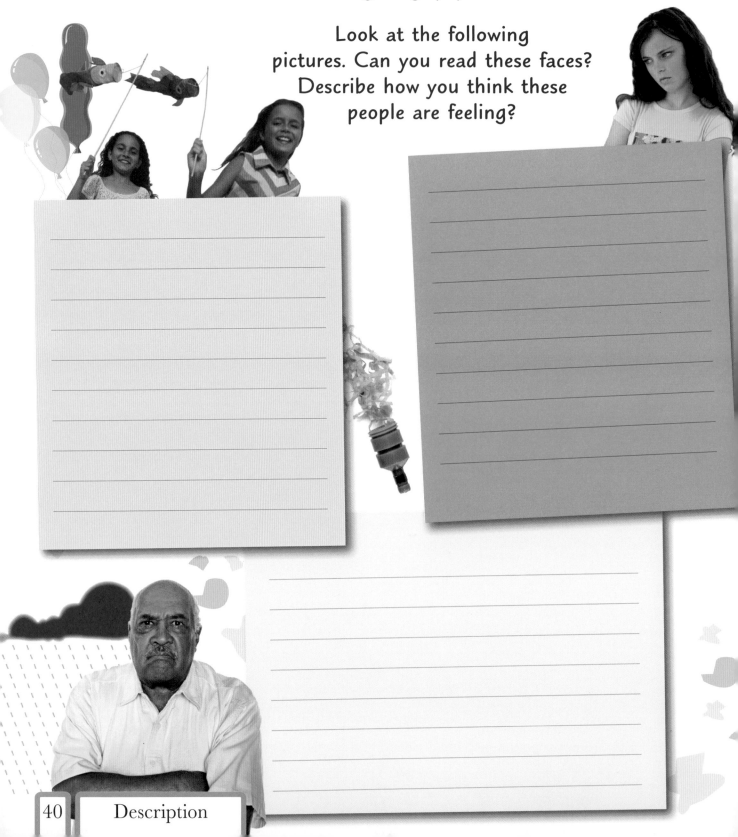

Description

Think of a time when you were bursting with emotion. Maybe you had just won a prize and were feeling proud; maybe you had a nightmare and were feeling scared.

CHALLENGE!
Use at least 5 synonyms to describe your emotion.

Write an account of what happened and include the different feelings you experienced at this time.

## WORD BOX

5 words to describe feelings:
1. delighted
2. cheerful
3. contented
4. ....................
5. ....................
   Add your own.

# The ordinary hero

Sometimes the greatest heroes of all are just ordinary people. Can you think of a time somebody you know came to the rescue?

Write a newspaper report about the day an ordinary person became a hero.

Write your headline at the top.

Who will be the hero of your story?

**CHALLENGE!**

Write a headline for your report that is so eye-catching your readers will want to read on!

What did they do? Who did they help?

Draw a picture of the hero in your report here.

What did eye-witnesses say about the event?

# Under the sea

Here's a writing challenge: tell an amazing underwater story with just 50 words. Dive in!

Start by drawing and planning your underwater scene.

What are the essential parts of the story?

**IT'S TRUE!**
More than 71 per cent of the Earth is covered by its oceans. There is much to explore!

Use only 50 words
to tell your story.

Make every word
work hard.

Tell your story to someone before you write it down.

What sea creatures are there?

What dangers lurk in the depths?

# Give us a clue

Priceless jewels have been stolen from the safe of a wealthy heiress. Whodunnit?

Write the clues that lead to how the jewels were stolen. Remember to ask yourself: who? what? when? why? where? how?

Who stole the jewels and why?

When did the crime take place?

What was the motive?

Write your red herring idea in here.

**CHALLENGE!**

Include a red herring! This is a misleading clue, which could make the reader think someone else did the crime.

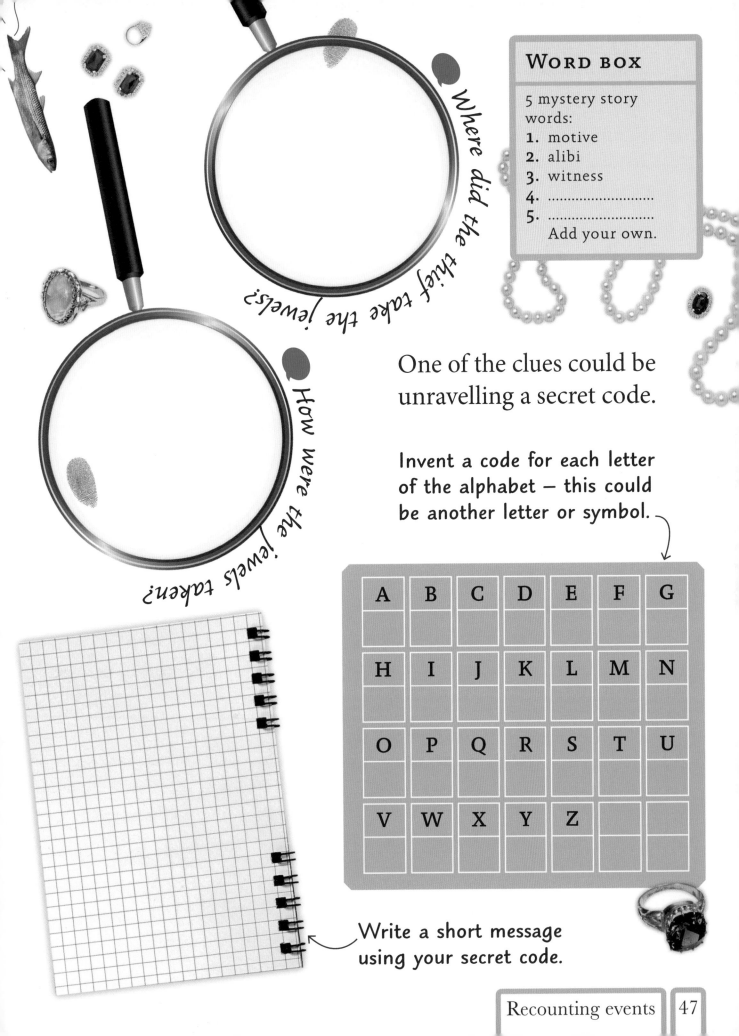

Where did the thief take the jewels?

How were the jewels taken?

## WORD BOX

5 mystery story words:
1. motive
2. alibi
3. witness
4. ......................
5. ......................
Add your own.

One of the clues could be unravelling a secret code.

Invent a code for each letter of the alphabet — this could be another letter or symbol.

| A | B | C | D | E | F | G |
|---|---|---|---|---|---|---|
|   |   |   |   |   |   |   |
| H | I | J | K | L | M | N |
|   |   |   |   |   |   |   |
| O | P | Q | R | S | T | U |
|   |   |   |   |   |   |   |
| V | W | X | Y | Z |   |   |
|   |   |   |   |   |   |   |

Write a short message using your secret code.

# Alien encounter

Imagine meeting a friendly alien from another planet. How would you greet the alien?

Draw a picture of the alien and its world.

What would your alien look like?

Where is the alien from?

...ite the start of a conversation between you ...d the alien. What will you find out about ...h other?

Use the yellow speech bubbles for your words.

Use the green speech bub for the alien's words.

What would you want to know about the alien's life?

What would you tell the alien about your life?

Dialogue

# Begin a legend

A legend is a traditional story about a particular person, animal or place. It is based on facts, but not completely true.

Robin Hood

Draw or make notes about where your legend is set.

● What will your legend be about?

King Arthur

Hercules

● Do you know these legends?

Unicorn

Excalibur

Legends begin by setting the time and place or introducing the character.

*There once lived a young boy...*

*Long ago, in a land far away...*

*How will you begin your legend?*

*In a place long forgotten...*

Write the beginning of your legend.

● *How is your character heroic?*

● *What makes the place intriguing?*

Leave your story unfinished, but at a point when the reader wants to know what happens next.

## WORD BOX

5 heroic verbs in past and present tense:
1. leap/leapt
2. fight/fought
3. creep/crept
4. ride/rode
5. vanquish/vanquished

Story openings

# Holiday news

Design a postcard for your best friend about an amazing, imaginary holiday you're having.

WORD BOX

5 adverbs to put in your postcard:
1. happily
2. lazily
3. boldly
4. ...........................
5. ...........................
Add your own.

*Life's a beach!*

*Where are you? What have you seen?*

*What was the weather like?*

Decorate the postcard with drawings and stickers.

*Wish you were here...*

Write on the back, telling them
what exciting things you've done.

Describe the food you ate?

How did you get there?

Add a sticker stamp here.

Have you seen any amazing animals?

Don't forget to add
their address here.

# High seas dilemma

Imagine you are a pirate captain. You are caught in a storm and your ship is sinking. Your ship is laden with treasure, but your crew want to abandon the ship and save themselves, leaving the treasure behind.

In your logbook, write five different options you could take.

What would you do if you were: greedy, caring, proud or daring?

Conflicts are gripping moments in a story. These happen when characters clash because they have different views. These events challenge characters and may change them.

Choose one of the options. Write what happens next here.

Include why you chose this option.

What are the results of your decision?

How are you and the crew affected?

**CHALLENGE!**

If a sea monster appeared, how would this affect your decision?

# Imaginary lands

Maps start to tell stories.

Create your own land.

Draw a map.

Label the places and landmarks.

What sort of country is this?

NEXT
4 MILES

Are there any dangerous areas?

| | 8 | 9 | 10 | 11 |
|---|---|---|---|---|
| a | | | | |
| b | | | | |
| c | | | | |
| d | | | | |

| 7 | 8 | 9 | 10 | 11 |

## WORD BOX

5 landmarks you
could include:
1. mountains
2. volcano
3. desert
4. .............................
5. .............................
   Add your own.

Is it a pleasant place to be?

Make some notes
about the land
you have imagined.

# Double life

Imagine someone you know has a secret… a very surprising job! Is the person an aunt, uncle or a grandparent? What are their characters like?

Draw the person in everyday clothes.

Now draw the same person in their secret job.

What job will it be: a fearless deep-sea diver; a heroic spy?

Write about the double life
of your chosen person.

*What are they like when you meet them?*

*What must they be like when they're doing their secret job?*

## WORD BOX

5 interesting words
for characters:
1. adventurous
2. daring
3. courageous
4. ingenious
5. shrewd
   Use a thesaurus
   to find some more.

**TOP SECRET**

# Comic strips

Comic strips are a fun way to tell a story.

Here is an example of a comic strip.

WHAM!

WORD BOX

5 exclamations for sound effects:
1. ZAP!
2. ZWOOSH!
3. OUCH!
4. ...Krak......
5. ...Chunk......
Add your own.

THE BUILDING IS ON FIRE. SCAREDY CAT NEEDS RESCUING!

SUPERDOG TO THE RESCUE!

THANKS SUPERDOG!

Add some dramatic colours.

Story openings

Create the opening of a story
in the style of a comic.

Who are your characters? What will they do?

What will your characters think and say?

Remember sound effects
and speech bubbles.

# Space adventure

Your spaceship has landed and you have just set foot on planet Mars. If you could send a message back to people on Earth, what would you tell them about the planet?

Write about the experience you are having in your message.

Describe the surface.

Is it hard? Is it soft, or maybe even bouncy?

Description

Remember, the more detail you give your readers, the better they can picture it in their minds! Use adjectives, similes and metaphors to extend your sentences.

CHALLENGE!
Pick one reason why the people of Earth should move to Mars. Try to make it very convincing!

Is there anything to eat?

What kinds of things can you see around you?

What is the temperature like?

# My time-travel diary

Write a diary of your time-travelling adventure.
Will you go back to a time in history or into the future?

Create a picture of the time you travel to.

What do the buildings look like?

What do people wear?

**CHALLENGE!**

What risks are there to time travelling and how would you overcome them?

How do you time travel? Is it by time machine or do you just go through a door?

Who do you see and meet?

Date:

Date:

What happens to you?

# Author to editor

You've written your amazing ideas for a story. You've improved your writing, using the best words and detail. So NOW it's time to check the story is ready for your readers. This process is called editing.

Your readers need to find your story easy to read or they'll just give up. This is why there are rules about how to write things down. Only by following the rules will they read it how you imagined it.

Top tip: Circle, underline or even use different coloured pencils to do the 3-step checks.

**Step 1. Grammar**

Why do it?

How will your readers follow the action of your story if the sentences are confusing?

Checklist:

☐ Have you stayed in the same tense throughout?

☐ Do the singular and plurals nouns and verbs agree?

☐ Does anything read awkwardly?

## Step 2. Spelling

Why do it?

How will your readers understand what's going on if words are spelt incorrectly?

Checklist:

- [ ] Have you used a dictionary or web-dictionary to find the correct spelling?

- [ ] Are apostrophes used correctly to show something belongs or in place of missing letters in contracted words?

Remember: put one line through the incorrect word and rewrite it — keep as neat as possible.

## Step 3. Punctuation

Why do it?

How will your readers make sense of your story if there's no punctuation to guide them?

Checklist:

- [ ] Are capital letters used at the beginning of each sentence and for names of characters, places and other proper nouns?

- [ ] Is there either a full stop, exclamation mark or a question mark at the end of every sentence?

- [ ] Have commas been used when short breaths are needed around clauses, in lists and before someone speaks?

- [ ] Are there speech marks around the words that the characters speak?

Remember: indent a word to start a new paragraph, when something new happens in the action, or someone begins to speak.

READY TO PUBLISH!

# Glossary

**account**
Written or spoken report about something that has happened.

**adjectives**
Words that describe a noun (person, place or thing), e.g. a *tiny* dog.

**adverbs**
Words that describe a verb (action word), an adjective or another adverb. Adverbs usually tell when, where, why or how something happened, often ending with –ly, e.g. *happily.*

**alliteration**
Words in a sentence that start with the same letter, e.g. *Tim's tiny tasty treat.*

**antonym**
Word that means the opposite to another word, e.g. *big is the antonym of small.*

**atmosphere**
Mood of a place or situation.

**character**
Person in a story, play or film.

**cliffhanger**
Dramatic, exciting incomplete ending of a chapter, leaving the readers wanting to read on and find out what happens next.

**climax**
Exciting or important event in a story.

**conflict**
Event that causes a disagreement or argument due to a difference of opinion between characters.

**connectives**
Word or phrase that links parts of a sentence to make a more complex one, e.g. *before; but also; next.*

**contraction**
Shortened forms of words formed by leaving out some letters, replacing them with an apostrophe, e.g. *do not – don't*

**dialogue**
Conversation between two or more people in a book, play or film.

**fairy tale**
Magical fantasy story, often with a happy ending.

**first-person story**
Written as from the character's or your own viewpoint, using the pronouns 'I' and 'we'.

**future tense**

Writing about an event that will happen or may happen, e.g. I *will be going* to the park tomorrow.

**legend**

Historical story that has been passed down over the years, but the facts have been altered and the characters made more or less heroic.

**metaphor**

Phrase that suggests a similarity between two different things, e.g. *the man is a snake*, meaning he is behaving in a snake-like way.

**method**

Step-by-step list of instructions to achieve or make something

**obstacle**

Something that blocks someone's way, preventing or hindering his/her progress, e.g. Sleeping Beauty's curse.

**paragraph**

Section in a piece of writing for when a new idea is introduced. Each section begins with an indented word.

**past tense**

Writing about an event that has happened already, e.g. I *went* to the shops yesterday.

**present tense**

Writing about an event as if it is happening now, e.g. I *am looking* in the window and I *see* a large cake.

**recount**

Telling a version of something that has happened.

**resolution**

Sorting out a conflict through an action or decision.

**rhetorical question**

Type of question that makes a point rather than needs an answer, e.g. *You are joking, aren't you?*

**setting**

Location where the action of a story, play or film takes place.

**simile**

Phrase that compares two different things, using 'as' or 'like', e.g. *she was as white as a sheet.*

**synonym**

Word that means exactly the same as another word, e.g. *happy, glad, joyful.*

**third-person story**

Written by a narrator telling the story, using the pronouns 'he', 'she' and 'they'.

# My story title

The title of a story is the hook for making the reader want to pick it up and read.

Here are some story themes. Think of some titles for each theme.

For example,
**Theme:** *ghost story*
**Titles:**
The Haunted House
Spooky Spine Chillers
The Dark, Dark Mansion

**Theme:** *mystery story*
**Titles:**

**Theme:** *alien story*
**Titles:**

**Theme:** *time-travel story*
**Titles:**

Which are your favourite story titles and why?

What will your theme be for your full-length story? Look back through this book for some ideas if you've not yet decided.

Note down some possible titles. Ask someone which title they prefer and why it would make them want to read the story.

Design a draft of a front cover with one of your titles.

Have a look at other book cover designs for inspiration!

# Planning my story

A blank page can be daunting when starting to write a story. Or your head may be buzzing with so many ideas that you're not sure where to start.

A great way to get ideas flowing is to prepare a story plan. It's like going up and down a mountain!

**Action**
_____
_____
_____
_____

**Setting**
_____
_____
_____
_____

**Opening**
_____
_____
_____
_____

**Climax**

_____

_____

_____

_____

You can start at any point, and go back to boxes as ideas start flowing and connecting.

**Conflicts**

_____

_____

_____

_____

**Resolution**

_____

_____

_____

_____

Who will be your main character? Who will oppose them?

Note down ideas for your characters' names.

Describe each of your characters here. How will they be different from each other? Draw them if you wish.

Which characters will have lesser roles?

My characters

Draft a conversation between some of the characters.
Try to convey their distinctive characters to the reader
in the dialogue.

Who is funny? Who asks questions? Who suggests ideas?

Who is the leader? Who gets emotional or excited?

*Where will your story take place?*
*Is there more than one location?*

Draw a map or plan of the places. Make the drawing as detailed as you need.
Add labels.

Note down phrases describing each place and its atmosphere.

How could you extend these phrases into longer sentences, using similes or metaphors?

My story openings

How will you hook your readers right from the start? Will you start with dialogue to set up the characters, create an atmosphere about the place, or leap straight into the action?

Draft your story opening here.

How does your opening reflect the type of story you'll be writing?

What details and words could you add to improve the opening further?

Reread it through or read it to someone.
Are you/they hooked?

How will the action grip your readers? Will your writing be scary, exciting or daring? What will happen?

Draft a piece for the climax of your story.

What is the main character's challenge?

How do the other characters react?

Stop the piece on a cliffhanger.

What will make a good ending for your story?
What needs to be resolved?

Draft your ending here.

How do you want your readers to feel at the end?

How have the characters changed from the start of your story?

Will you end on a happy or funny sentence, or leave the readers with something to think about?

# My story

You've plotted and planned, discussed and drafted. NOW the moment has come to start writing your story. Pen or pencil at the ready! Chapter One, here you come!

Title: .................................................

This story was written by:

.................................................

On: ...............................................

At: ................................................

With thanks to: ...........................

.................................................

.................................................

My story

My story

My story

My story

My story

My story

My story

**DK** | Penguin Random House

**Senior Editor** Deborah Lock
**Editor** Katy Lennon
**Assistant Editor** Méabh Collins
**Project Art Editor** Hoa Luc
**Designer** Emma Hobson
**Art Director** Martin Wilson
**Publisher** Laura Buller
**Producer, Pre-production** Francesca Wardell

**Consultant** Jacqueline Harris

First published in Great Britain in 2015
by Dorling Kindersley Limited
80 Strand, London, WC2R 0RL

Copyright © 2015 Dorling Kindersley Limited.
A Penguin Random House Company
15 16 17 18 19 10 9 8 7 6 5 4 3 2 1
001–284612–Sept/2015

A CIP catalogue record for this book
is available from the British Library
ISBN: 978-0-2412-0685-0

Printed and bound in China.

The publisher would like to thank Leah Panigada-Carey for the illustration on page 60 and
Catherine Saunders for proof-reading.
The publisher would like to thank the following
for their kind permission to reproduce their photographs:
(Key: a-above; b-below/bottom; c-centre; f-far; l-left; r-right; t-top)

**Alamy Images:** Alaska Stock / Design Pics Inc 52fbr; Atomazul 38bl; Michael Burrell 12-13; Judith
Collins 1fbr, 9br; Jeremy Cozannet 1fcrb (gorilla), 9crb; Mim Friday 8br; Fritz, Gerard F. / SuperStock
44clb; D. Hurst 1ftl (rocket), 48fcl; Jupiterimages / Pixland 40cra; Khaled Kassem 9tr; KQS / Stockimo
92-93 (background); Kuligssen 34; Emmanuel Lattes 27fcra, 66c; Lisa Moore 4br; The Print Collector
50fcr; Pongphan Ruengchai 29cl; Ingo Schulz / imagebroker 6ftr; Dmytro Skorobogatov 84-85
(background); Anton Starikov 76ca; Sergii Telesh 54-55 (book); Andrzej Tokarski 43tl; Wegler, M. /
Juniors / Juniors Bildarchiv GmbH 43tr; A. T. Willett 88-89 (background). **Corbis:** 53b; 145 / Anthony
Bradshaw / Ocean 28fbl; Apolonia / Masterfile 38br; Caspar Benson / fstop 80-81 (background); Rolf
Hicker / All Canada Photos 2bl, 59fbl; Steven Krug 82-83 (background); Elisa Lazo de Valdez 15br;
John Lund / Blend Images 54-55; Oleksiy Maksymenko / age fotostock Spain S.L. 32br; Yva Momatiuk &
John Eastcott / Minden Pictures 58bc; Ned Frisk Photography 40bl; Thomas Roepke 38cla; TongRo
Images 2fbl (food), 27br; Martin van Lokven / NiS / Minden Pictures 34tc. **Dorling Kindersley:**
4hoplites 10b; The American Museum of Natural History 1ca (arrow), 1cra, 1cr (arrow), 50cla, 50cra;
Anthony Barton Collection 37clb; Banbury Museum 64fcl; Blandford Fashion Museum 59cla, 64ftr;
James Brunker / Rough Guides 52cla; Cecil Williamson Collection 22bc, 23l; Chateau de Saumur 36cla;
Cotswold Farm Park; Gloucestershire 36fbl; Ian Cuppleditch 2fcl (plant), 56fcl, 57fbr; Tim Draper /
Rough Guides 1ftl (moon), 6fcla, 34br, 48bl, 67fbr; Durham University Oriental Museum 46tr; Neil
Fletcher 41fcra (bee); Curtis Hamilton / Rough Guides 26bl; Chas Howson / Court of Chancery Hoard,
Courtesy of The British Museum / The Trustees of the British Museum 2cb (coins), 50fcla (coins); Claire
Cordier 56fbl; Lindsey Stock 7br; Twan Leenders 33crb (frog); Thomas Marent 2fbr (frog), 6bc, 73bl
(frog); Museo Archeologico Nazionale di Napoli 35ca; Natural History Museum, London 1bl (butterfly),
1fcr (butterfly), 21cr, 47fbr; Roger Norum / Rough Guides 2fclb, 58bl; Stephen Oliver 2ftl (compass),
19cr (pencil sharpener), 30br, 57fcra; Gary Ombler / Whipple Museum of History of Science,
Cambridge 2ftl (timer), 65tr; Chester Ong 4c, 5c, 35c, 36c, 38cla (background), 38cra (background),
38bl (background), 38br (background), 39c; Order of the Black Prince 36br; Suzanne Porter / Rough
Guides 2bc (rock), 33ftr, 53bc; The Science Museum, London 8bl, 65br; The Shuttleworth Collection
59fcra, 73btr; Natascha Sturny / Rough Guides 52ca (chapel), The University of Aberdeen 33ftr (coin),
33fcrb (coin); University of Pennsylvania Museum of Archaeology and Anthropology 33cr (coin);
Martin van Lokven / NiS / Minden Pictures 67fcrb; Wallace Collection, London 37cla, 37crb; Greg
Ward / Rough Guides 35tr; Weymouth Sea Life Centre 2fcla, 47ftl, 72ftr (fish). **Dreamstime.com:**
Andreus 64cla; Andrew7726 38cb, 38fcra, 38fcr, 38fclb, 39tc, 39fcrb, 39fbr; Roberto Atencia Gutierrez
/ Roberaten 74cl, 74bc, 74br; Alexander Babich / Suricoma 16bc; Mircea Bezergheanu / Bereta 8fcla;
Bolotov 1bc (paper), 1fbr (paper), 2bc (paper); Roman Borodaev / Borodaev 74tr; Yuriy Chaban / Dja65
3br, 50bl; Ron Chapple / Iofoto 11b; Chee Siong Teh / Tehcheesiong 16c (bucket); Lucy Clark /
Quackersnaps 10bl; Cynoclub 44bc; Karl Daniels / Webphoto99 45br; Dvmsimages 2tr (cogs), 65t,
65ftr, 72br; Edonalds 24c, 25; Ensuper 50cla (background), 50bc (background), 50bc (background),
50br (background), 50fclb (background); Gearstd 73crb; Ilya Genkin / Igenkin 45c; Walter Graneri /
Argironeta 16fcr; Paul Hakimata / Phakimata 69tc; Imagery Majestic / Imagerymajestic 59fcrb;
Sataporn Jiwjalaen / Onairjiw 6c; Kess 26c, 76br; Carl Keyes / Ckeyes888 22cr; Christopher King /
Wingnutdesigns 61c; Klikk 57tr; Konstanttin 51tl; Jakub Krechowicz / Sqback 23; Kuanchong Ng /
Kuanchong 27bc; Lekchangply 2fbl (bottle), 28br; Olga Lyubkin 4bc; Robyn Mackenzie / Robynmac
24bl; Marbenzu 50fbr; Mcarrel 18cl; Paul Moore / Diomedes66 15cra; Stanko Mravljak / Stana 52br;

Nexus7 15c; Oneo 5br; Pakhnyushchyy 47bl, 68tr, 68br, 69tl, 69r, 78; Anita Patterson Peppers /
Anitapatterson 11bl; Peeterson 1fbl (atlas), 50fbl; Rangizzz 37c; Julián Rovagnati / Erdosain 41fcra;
Scorpion26 52bl; Radu Sebastian / Sebalos 1br (ship), 54bl; Shishkin 2tl (lights), 58-59t; Asther Lau
Choon Siew / Pufferfishy 44fbl; Silvionka 26tr; Jason Stitt / Keeweeboy 21bl; Eti Swinford /
Littlemacproductions 65bl; Martin Valigursky / Mvaligursky 16cr; Ronald Van Der Beek / Uzuri 1ftl
(camera), 48cl (camera); Vilmos Varga / Medveh 1bl (gecko), 39fcr; Vrozhko 86-87 (background);
Aizhong Wang / Zhengzaishanchu 55bc, 73fbr; Wangyun 90-91 (background); Waxart 16br; Yael Weiss
3cla, 3c, 3clb, 46cra, 46cl, 46bl, 47tc, 47cl, 72ftr; Jamie Wilson / Jamiewilson 48br, 72fclb; Simone
Winkler / Eyecatchlight 4l; Zygotehasnobrain 77, 79. **Fotolia:** Auris 20br; Beboy 35b; dundanim 2tc,
49tr; electriceye 10cl; Alexey Repka 25ftr; Tomislav 31bl; uwimages 44bl. **National Science Foundation,
USA:** Ethan Norris 58b.

**Jacket images:** *Front:* **Alamy Images:** Michael Burrell fcla/ (book); Ingo Schulz / imagebroker ftl.
**Dorling Kindersley:** James Brunker / Rough Guides fcra/ (beach); Cecil Williamson Collection fbl;
Natural History Museum, London tl. **Dreamstime.com:** Ilya Genkin / Igenkin br; Carl Keyes /
Ckeyes888 bl; Stanko Mravljak / Stana fcra/ (snow); Scorpion26 ftr/ (camera). **Fotolia:** Auris fcrb. *Back:*
**Alamy Images:** Sergii Telesh cl/ (book); Wegler, M. / Juniors / Juniors Bildarchiv GmbH ftr. **Dorling
Kindersley:** Chas Howson / Court of Chancery Hoard, Courtesy of The British Museum fclb/ (coins);
Stephen Oliver tc; The University of Aberdeen fclb/ (coin 1); University of Pennsylvania Museum of
Archaeology and Anthropology fclb/ (coin 2). **Dreamstime.com:** Dvmsimages ftl; Walter Graneri /
Argironeta fcra/ (forest); Martin Valigursky / Mvaligursky fcra/ (water); Yael Weiss br.

All other images © Dorling Kindersley
For further information see: www.dkimages.com

A WORLD OF IDEAS:
SEE ALL THERE IS TO KNOW
www.dk.com

## Note to Parents/Carers

This book is designed to help children write their own stories and
to provide support for the writing process. Each activity develops
a slightly different skill and allows children to experiment with
different styles and ideas before writing their own story in the final
pages. The activities can be done in any order.

The word boxes and challenges are designed to encourage
children to stretch their ideas and vocabulary, and use more
technical words when relevant. If they have a dictionary,
they can use five minutes at the end of each activity to check
their spellings. It is best to let children have a go at spelling first
and view corrections as part of the editing process as this
enables their ideas to flow. You could suggest they just put a line
under words they are not sure how to spell and then look them
up at the end, or you could help them with the spelling of the
trickier words. This enables children to be more independent
and encourages them to use more challenging vocabulary
rather than being anxious over spelling every word correctly
first time.

The talking points are an essential part in the writing
process. Children can try out ideas and discuss their
thoughts with an adult, friend or sibling, clarifying any
points before starting to write them down. This helps
enormously if they don't know what to write at first.
Encourage children to vocalise what they are going to write
and if they come up with any great words or phrases to
quickly jot them down so they don't forget them.

This book will enable your children to practise the
elements involved in creating stories and to experience
writing as a pleasurable, imaginative process.